Head over Heart

Head over Heart

Poetry Collection
About Love, Happiness,
and Emotions

ANRAN LIKEN

To order additional copies of this book, contact:
Xlibris
844-714-8691
www.Xlibris.com
Orders@Xlibris.com
816900

Contents

Just You

I just want to hold you in my arms
kiss away your sorrows whilst telling you
with my love that it is all right

Hold so tight till the lonely feeling fades
into the mist, never to return
opening your heart to receive the love
that is given so freely, only wanting you
to love it in return

Giving only you, your time, your joy
will always bring the heart of your choice
a heart that wants just you and only you
others interfere but cannot take away
what is true

Be true to yourself, and she whom you await
will be yours all the sooner; by showing
just your heart, you win her heart in return
for she just wants the man, not what he can
give her in material things

See You

I see your face,
my heart skips a beat,
love blooms,
hope blossoms,
dreams of what would be,
visions of what might be,
glances in images' eyes,
falling deeper,
loving evermore.

Passion Awaits

She sits waiting, thinking about
what it would be like to lie with you,
feel your skin with her hands,
softly touching, sliding down your body,
feeling you tremble.

When she reaches your sensitive parts,
you wait, pleading silently for her not to stop.
She senses your held breath,
smiles, for she knows now where
you need to be touched.

She teases you, making you catch your breath
deeper, making you want her to go further,
pushing you harder,
making you cry out something you've never done before.
Why with her?

You want her, but she will not let you touch her.
She wants you to enjoy first.
She is doing things that others have done,
but with her, they are more,
more than just going through emotions.

She stops just when you don't want her to.
Looking in your eyes, she sits on top of you,
sliding down your shaft so slowly
that you almost explode.
She is so tight; you just want to take her.

She unties your hands.
You take hold of her.
Turning her over, you thrust into her.
She's taking you deeper than anyone before,
holding on to you, crying out with each.

A tear falls from your eye on to her face.
She wipes away your tears, kissing you
with passion, taking you each time,
telling you with her eyes that she is here
for you and only you.

Falling on to her breasts, both crying together.
The passion and emotions are too much.
She kisses away your tears,
saying 'I love you',
and no one has ever made you
feel so complete.

Moments

I love you in a million ways
never knowing how to tell you
not wanting to scare you

Tensely hoping not to offend you
you say it first; I am speechless that a
man so great could love a woman like me

Moments come, moments go
the right moments are here
forever

Memories made, memories taken
lasting a lifetime
cherished for evermore

Watching

I watch you from the other side of the screen
wishing, hoping
you are too far to reach
each moment, watching
wanting to reach out and
touch you
the next, the last
never will it end
wanting, feeling
pushing emotions
deeper inside till
that moment you look
and finally speak it
out loud: 'I love that man'
only to have no answer
silence, speaking back
at you, only the voice
from the screen speaking in code

Secret Love

A secret love hidden deep beneath
no one to see the struggle
of hiding from him
distance is no different in
time of miles

He never knows you are waiting
only a single pray given
never listened to
hoping, never wishing
maybe someday

Using your secret love
to help with your pain
using it to believe there is hope
left in the world
never knowing, believing,
hoping that one day
dreams might come true

Chasing Rainbows

Always chasing rainbows
pot of gold at the end, raining
the sun is shining, looking for the rainbow
clouds of grey, white fluffy pillows

Cupid playing, bow pulled, arrow ready
to fly across the sky, set the stars on fire
shimmering glow of red, blue
purple, golden yellow

Sun rising, chasing grey clouds away
blue skies
not a cloud up ahead
but what is that?
a wet drop on the face

Is that rain? looking round at the sky
hoping to see clouds of grey
but nothing to see
there it is again
another drop

Do you hear that?
what? no
'tis like a bell tolling, but like a cry too
all rolled into one
what can it be?

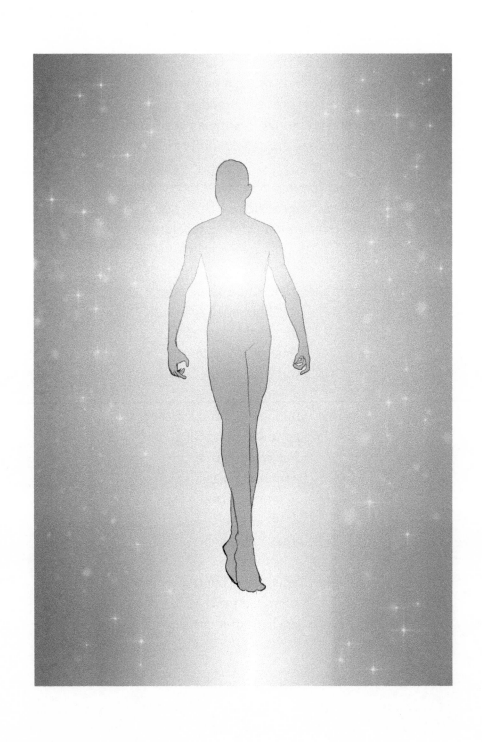

Blind Faith

Your pain is like a
hunger, eating away at your soul
life will never be the same again
or so it may seem

You scream and shout at her
for not wanting to help any more
is she really who you want
in your world if she cannot help?

You thought she was someone special
someone who would be there for you
in every way possible

She let you down at the last hurdle
just one hurdle out of them all
that you had placed in front of her

I know who I am, but she does not
I am asking her to believe with blind faith
without giving something back of myself

She has believed in everything
I have said and asked
given all that she can
and for me, it is still
not enough; she has to
prove to me some more

For I find it hard to trust now
past situations made it so
she has had the same, but still
she has given on blind faith

All she has done was done on blind faith
I let her down by not believing in her
I didn't have blind faith
I just demanded

Act of Chance

One moment in time can change a life
Seconds change a moment into a chance
It is a look, a word, a touch of a hand, a melding of minds
Twining of hands of beating hearts loving
each other from far-off lands
Oceans, in between chances of waves, reach for the stars
Moonlight sparkles as tears fall down from
the clouds as chances missed
Laughter sprinkles hope into the cracks
Bringing chances shimmering to life
New growth of hope

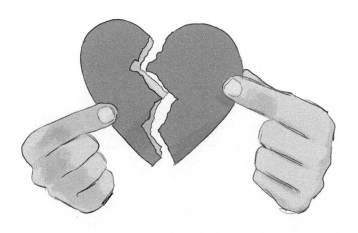

Broken

My heart is oh-so filled with love for you
every moment spent thinking
a light has returned
lighting the spark, once so dim, almost
lost in the dark

Broken heart, the fire almost gone
passion dimming with every flame
that is extinguished, nothing left
to heal the wounds

A star is shining, healing light reaching out
to bridge the vastness of empty wounds
stitching together pieces of a jigsaw

Sealing the jagged edges of broken flesh
bringing together the faith and trust
honesty leading the way forward

Healing a broken heart
bringing passion and fire back
light burning so brightly
blinding the heart into beating
first love

Angel's Love

You lie beside her, watching her breathing
kissing gently on her eyes
trailing down to her lips
she smiles, feeling your touch
caressing

Opening her eyes, looking into yours
she reaches for you
taking hold of your face
making the kiss deeper
taking and giving, wanting you more

She opened her heart to you
giving her love freely
you took everything she offered
never giving a thought to
giving it back

You lie there, looking at a space
that was once so full
where she lay
you reach, stroking that side
wondering why

You see her everywhere
wanting her to be back in your arms
but she turns away
when you try to talk
not seeing her tears

You never looked into her soul
you never really saw that that was her
for if you had
you would see you have lost
the love of an angel

You

You brought the meaning of life to
a broken heart with calming words
healing hands

Gently covering slivers of jagged flesh
softly caressing the wounds
sealing tethered ends

Once again, a broken heart in need
of your shoulders, your
calming, loving words
hands that healed

Gone is the pain, the weight that was
holding down the broken heart
will hold no more
Lightness of heart, healing once more
control of life is gone, to yours once more
it shall be

A Mother's Love

She carried you for nine months
through the sickness, tiredness
aching bones in her body

Her pain of joy at seeing your face
tears running down a mother's face
loving you in an instant

Never giving up hope for wonderful things
you will want to endure everything
that life has to give to you

Each night you never heard the crying
for the love lost for her
the hatred she saw in your eyes

Not understanding what she had done
or where she had gone wrong
but just giving a mother's love
is all that she can give

Summer Nights

Waiting for long summer nights
sitting on the beach, watching the sun set
hoping that you will maybe
next time be with someone

You see other couples wrapped in blankets
cuddling together, keeping warm, watching
the sun set

Fires burning, lighting up the night
the smell of burning wood
tingling the senses, watching
everyone settling in to watch the stars

You turn to go, collecting your things
colliding with a hard structure
not looking where you are going
as tears in your eyes blind you

Looking up into blue-green eyes
you apologise
he takes hold to steady you
your skin burns from his touch
shimmering down to your toes

You try to move away yet do not want to
but to be held by him, why him? a stranger
when the one who should be holding you
is with another

He sees your pain, moves away
but then takes hold of your face
between his hands, wiping your tears
taking your lips ever so slowly

Moving in closer, you want more of him
this stranger, in minutes
has made you feel so much more
than you have ever felt in a lifetime

Waiting for long summer nights
along the beach, watching
the sun set with strangers
who become lovers

Angel of Hope

You came to me like an angel from the heavens
I thought I was dreaming
why would he want to have
anything to do with me?

He calls me beautiful
why? I do not know
I am just me
a woman
just wanting to be loved

Unbelieving of what is asked or said
told too many lies to trust
always has faith
but is never believing

You hold out the hand of friendship
with nothing
but a smile in your eyes
asking to be trusted

Taking hold of your smile
I begin to open my heart
feeling warmth encase it
beginning to trust again
having faith in what I see
what I believe in

Wanting To Be Number One

Sitting on my bed, talking and chatting with you, I feel at peace
Then you change it up
you think I am rich; you think I am something more
I'm not; I'm just a woman wanting
to be friends, trying to be friends

Always charities this, charities that
can you just spare this? can you just spare that?
I'm not a rich woman; I am a widow who just
wants to be loved, just wants to be put first
for once in her life, instead of being second
or third or fourth

I just want to be someone's number one
the first thing they think about before going to bed
or waking up in the morning
that makes your heart melt when
my face pops into your head

But no, again I'm never enough
I'm never good enough for that or anyone
I often wonder why I was put on this earth
why did I live?
why am I here at all?

Dreams of Wanting

Wanting to lie with you beside me, feeling
your warm skin pressing against mine
holding your arms around my body
keeping me tight and close to your heart

I feel you stirring, your hand moving, caressing
I turn to face you, reaching and kissing your eyes
trailing kisses until I reach your sweet lips

Feeling you smile as you return the kiss
making it deeper, more passionate
you start leaving kisses all over my body
whilst touching, holding

Taking hold of my hands so you can control the pace
stopping me from touching you, for you know
you cannot hold on when I caress you
leaving trails of love where I have touched

Finally, you've had enough feeding of me
you release my hands; I turn you over
taking you at the same time
you cry out, not able to hold on any more

Riding out the morning together
we collapse on to each other
holding on to the dream
just a little longer, hoping
it doesn't fade too quickly this time

Love One Another

Why are we so cruel to each other?
We are all on this earth for a reason
Each one of us with a gift to help one another

Love one another, for all that we can
Love one another, for this is who we are

Colour does not define who we are
For it is just a pigment in our skin
Pink, cream, brown, dark, chocolate, black

Love one another, just because we can
Love one another; this is who we are

Bullying of a person because of
His/her colour is wrong
For it does not make you powerful
But belittles who you could be

Love one another, love one another
Love one another, love the world as we should
Love one another as we would
Love one another as we could
Love one another, love one another

Key To A Loving Heart

You are the morning sun's warming cuddles rays,
that light the heart to begin a new day

The first thing that is in thy heart and head,
hoping for loves to blossom in a world

I love you when you are mad,
annoyed, angry, even sad
love as no boundaries,
love as no time or even limits

My love is for everyone,
when my heart falls in love
then she is timeless
you hold the key to my heart

Keep safe in your own heart
for you lose my key
you have lost my heart.

Movie Star

You are the star on the movie screen
adored by many, envied by most

Your piercing brown eyes look out
at your fans, each one hoping
you are looking at them

You read your lines, never missing a beat
ladies swoon in their seats, boyfriends
and husbands catch them where they fall

They look at you, thinking, *why
does she never do this for me?*
not understanding you are their
fantasy

The movie ends
you leave them wanting more
maybe next time
maybe nevermore

For the light is dimmer now
the sparkle is getting old
you want a life like everyone else
you want more
than just the life of a movie star

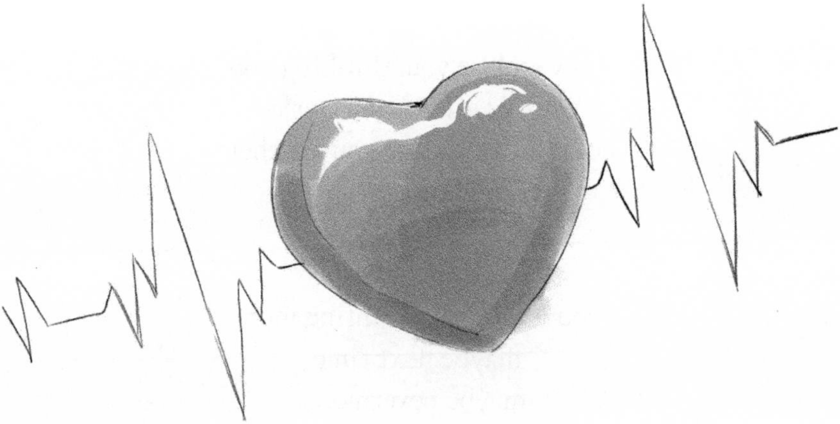

Hearts Are Beating

Heart is beating in time with breathing
however, it is not beating in time
with your heart, but his

Flying through the water
feeling free as the birds
the spray of droplets
sparkling like diamonds

Heart beating, with heat burning
for you feel her inside of your heart
pushing love through your veins

Hoping for the next wave to be the one
to bring you closer together
bodies tangling together

Rolling together, touching, feeling
every breath taken
every beat pulsing through veins
burning with love

My Bleeding Heart

My heart is breaking all over again,
it is hard to breathe for the pain of feeling it being torn apart,
each tear drawing more pain.

This emotional pain will fade away,
this wound will need someone with patience to help heal it,
believe that there is someone who wants just you.

Your pain is harder this time, for he was your true one,
you may never recover; only time will tell,
waiting is all you can hope for.

Letting go will take a lifetime,
no other will ever take his place,
forever having a bleeding heart of pain.

Belief

You ask the question, hoping for the answer
praying it will be the one
never hearing the right answer
wanting more and more
for it to be the answer

Looking out the window
watching the sea swirl round
thinking of going for a surf
white horses raging, crashing on the beach
just right for the long ride

Again looking, is there an answer?
not yet, no; when will it be?
just believe that it will be there, waiting
go catch the waves, clear your mind
brush the cobwebs away

Fighting the surf, gliding on the waves
turning, crossing, feeling the pull
you feel the knot in your stomach
crashing in the waves, you run

Light is flashing; is it from—? is it the answer?
no, you throw your phone away in disgust
head in your hands
wanting to cry but can't

A shadow crosses your path; you look up, see it is her
looking into her eyes, you know
the answer to your question, but
you still get down on bent knee
to ask

Putting a finger on your mouth
she looks into your eyes, whispering
'yes, I will marry you
for I cannot live without you
you are my world
my everything'

Brothers

Laid in, your billet rifle at the ready
half asleep, one eye open, others
sleeping, listening to sounds of the night

Boom, boom, boom, out of bed
uniform at the ready, rifle in arms
pack on back, chasing out the door

Helmets in hand
sweat dripping down faces
hard look in eyes
brothers not returning

Sharing of memories
laughing at each other
remembering of fallen brothers
drinking to their courage

Returning home with the fallen brothers
never leaving them behind
always got each other's backs

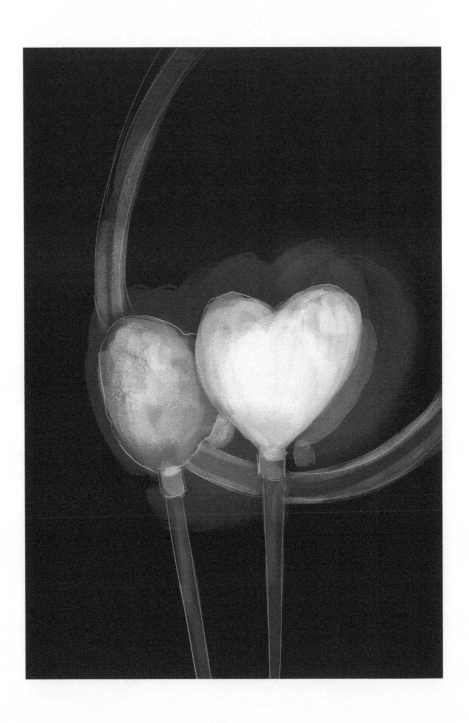

Light that Brightens

You are the light that brightens the shadows of the night
you creep in where no one dares to tread
giving hope for what might be

Moving through rivers of darkness
flowing through veins that need the light, returning
what once was lost through ignorance

Taking back what was lost; 'tis now found
pushing faster through beating to retrieve
the lost gem that was stolen all those years ago

Travelling deeper into the depths
of what was there; it is now here, waiting
for you to collect it, to lift the light out of the darkness

Taken from the shadows
the light burns through
wants to be seen more and more
pushing out of darkness
blasting into the silence's glare

9 781664 113091